Boldly Delicate

Sindhu Reddy

BookLeaf Publishing

India | USA | UK

Presentation by BookLeaf Publishing

Web: www.bookleafpub.com

E-mail: info@bookleafpub.com

ISBN: 9789395969352

First edition 2023

DEDICATION

This book is dedicated to my best friend, who has always been my biggest supporter and to everyone who always believed in me and also to those who did not because, your doubt has given me an opportunity to challenge myself and come this far in life. Thank you.

- The Author

ACKNOWLEDGEMENT

I would like to acknowledge BookLeaf Publishing for bringing this opportunity in my way to share my thoughts and time with the world. I would like to thank the very few people in my life who always push me forward with their encouragement and those who always clap for me and also those who have been silently supporting me all along the way. Without whom I would not have been able to find the strength to push through.

The truth always sets us free, no matter how it is released.

- The Author

PREFACE

'Boldly Delicate' is a collection of poems that mark my debut into the poetic world.
Even though I had a fair amount of experience as an imaginative and realistic writer both, poetry always seemed a bit daunting to me. Mainly because good poetry demands utmost honesty to self, even in the deepest of our imagination. But as I finally challenged myself and started writing poems, I realized that poems could be real, bold, and equally beautiful at the same time. Each poem has a different theme. Most are from my own experiences and emotions, while some are from the interactions which left a lasting impact on my thought process. This journey has been nothing but therapeutic and has made me realize that it is possible to inspire by anything and anyone to face our own inner truth and express it through our poems. Hope you have a good read!

-The Author

Love in Instalments

"Time is money", someone had said to her.
So she spent her time, whatever she had left to
pay him back
He had loaned her out his heart
Here she was, paying it back in full and with
interest.
The instalments are set to go on,
for a period of "lifetime"
For there cannot be a price put on "Love"
but can only be repaid with more love.

Just Fine

He asked her, "How are you holding up ?"
She looked up, as his gaze met her eyes
Eyes that were tired from not sleeping amidst
the chaos every night
Chaos that came from the noises not around
her, but inside her.
These noises were from all the shattering
pieces of her delicate heart.
Her heart heavy from all the emptiness it wakes
up to every morning, she let out a sigh
Then took a deep breath, as deep as the place
she goes to
Everyday, to drown her silence
and said,
"Oh, I am doing just fine ".

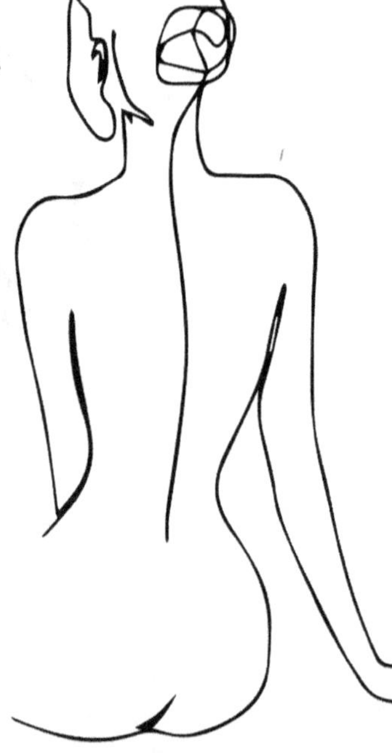

The One

She who could not decide what to eat had decided it was him.
How did she know?
When everyone else was just looking at her pictures,
He was listening, listening to the story behind them.
When rest of the men wanted her to be their trophy,
he wanted her to be herself and happy.
Before trying to reach her lips like the rest of them,
he reached out to kiss her eyes first.
While rest of them loved what she had to offer,
he offered his heart to her.
While rest of them lusted after the woman she had become,
he saw through her to find a little girl searching for love.
While rest of them were talking about "how great her goods were",
he gazed into her eyes listening to the silence in them.
That's how she knew, "It was him".

Believe her

*Before you ask her to "Stop Overthinking",
remember that there was a time she had the
brightest smile
Eyes that shone even brighter when she spoke
about the things she loved.
These were the things she loved before she was
broken,
broken in so many different ways that she was
constantly thinking
Thinking if she "should do it" or "speak about
it" for everything she ever did
So many times, until she almost convinced
herself that she'd never be good at anything
Anything, that she otherwise would have gone
through with, in a heartbeat.
and anything which she always loved to say or
do
Yet, she ends up not going through with most of
them
Even with you and everyone around her
cheering on,
cheering on knowing the best of her and how
well she can.
So when she repeatedly asks you about
something,*

*know that you are someone she trusts more
than her own thoughts.*
The next time you see her, reassure her
*Reassure her thoughts, showing her you
believe in her*
Believe her more than she believes herself
Believe her that she can.

Puzzle

She was putting together a picture
The picture was a portrait.
A portrait of her life scattered all over,
very few were right before her while most were
hidden
Some pieces were in her past, scattered down
memory lane
Some were in her present but buried,
buried deep under the rumbles of pain
The pain caused by the burdening weight of
expectations, opinions and judgements
from her own kin
Some more could be found hanging from a
cracked corner of her heart
There she was, carefully picking them up and
trying to piece them back together
Together to make herself whole,
Her life was just one piece short
So she pulled one out of her heart and became
whole again
The next time she says, "You are my missing
piece", know that "You are her heart".

Man up

A little boy he was,
who had eyes that gleamed with joy and
curiosity
Curiosity, that had questions eager to find
answers
Those eyes carried racing dreams and beautiful
desires
There he was, becoming a man
"Be a protector", they said
"Be successful", they said
"Be responsible for your partner", they said
"Men don't cry", they said
but most importantly, " Man up", they said.
He was turning into a man whose curious eyes
were now growing tired,
tired from all the heavy burden of
"responsibilities"
When you see him this time,
let his heart pour out as you let the burden rest
on your shoulders.
And for a little while,
protect his heart.

Wings

Let her fly,
fly as high as the blue sky with her dreams
made into wings
Wings as broad as the doorway to her desires
Her deepest desires, kept safe
tucked away as little wishes
These wishes, she hides from the world
Some from herself too
They sometimes roll down her cheeks when the
stardust of her dreams falls back in her eyes
When she's tired, she looks for a place,
a place she can rest her feet and fix her wings
A place she can go back to again
Let her come home,
let your arms be her home.

Home

"Where were you?" asked her mother
There she was, Standing at the door with a cold gaze,
As cold as the winters,
winters of a place which was now her home
It was merely a place to rest,
to rest her body but not her heart.
She heads out everyday in hope,
of running into her home
It being a place she can rest
A place she can put down her heavy burden,
wash her sorrows down,
let her guard down to take off the layers covering her
soul, one by one
Until her soul is stripped naked, so she can cuddle
under a warm blanket
The blanket made from a pair of arms,
the arms of someone she calls 'Home'.

She

"Be simple", they said
When she was actually simple," She is too plain,"
they said.
"Be bold," they said.
When she was honest enough, "She's too bitchy,
"they said.
"Be nice and friendly, " they said
When she tried to be a good friend, "Stop leading
guys on," they said.
"Be independent, "they said
When she had opinions, "She's too difficult," they
said.
"Earn money," they said
When her skill gave her confidence," She is too
headstrong, " they said.
'She' is not a weight to be balanced on a scale but a
part of 'you'
The next time you see her, take off your colored
glasses, so you can see how colourful her world is.

The 'Clown Friend'

She was the 'clown friend'
The friend who was always fun
'The entertainer' of the group.
The one who was supposed to act dumb
The one supposed to be 'always happy',
happy no matter what was on the inside.
One day she stopped,
Stopped being what she was supposed to be,
only to start being 'her'
Started speaking her heart, only to see her own
people leave her
The more she started being honest, the less they
wanted her
She watched in silence as the people she 'knows'
slowly became ones she 'knew',
as their once 'clown friend' was now 'too boring'.

Her World

"What do you want from life ?" he asked.
"I want to run,
I want to stumble,
I want to fly,
I want to learn,
I want to travel,
I want to love and be loved,
I want to be rich,
rich with all the things right in the world.
I want to build my own little paradise in that world.
But most importantly, I want you
to be a part of the same world,
as the best place for my world seems to be your
heart,"
screamed her insides.
"I just don't know yet," replied her lips.

Him

What does he look like?
"He has beautiful eyes, those I want to get lost in
Lips that plant soft kisses, softer than his heart
itself
A smile I want to be a reason for
Arms, big enough to wrap me in a warm hug,
one which feels like home
A chest I could rest my head to feel his heartbeat,
Whose rhythm echoes in my ears, even from afar,
The one in which I search my name
Hands that hold mine as if, too precious to let go
He to me is 'Perfect'.

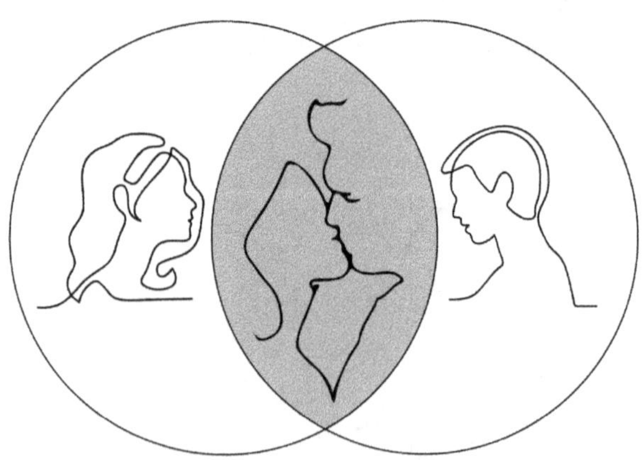

The Red velvet Cake

She walked down the street
Passing by the Baker's,
smelling of sweet delights as sweet as her smile
Croissants as soft and warm as her heart,
bagels as different as her personality
Chocolates that looked like sparkly pieces of
words wrapped up in bits of her joy
Candies that shone like her eyes, sparkling
when she spoke of things she loved
She stopped, to pick up a piece of cake
Layered, just like her, with each layer,
as beautiful as her soul
There it was, a piece of her favourite
'The Red velvet Cake'.

Dark

"Come home before its dark", her mother's
words echoed in her ears
She jolted out and found herself sleeping,
Sleeping away amidst the racing thoughts
Thoughts, sometimes being as they are,
or those that manifested,
manifested into reality
A reality, everchanging,
one she never intended to be a part of
Rather, she came to realize now,
that this was a part of her
It ran through her veins,
reaching into her soul
consuming her, bit by bit
Now she could see in true sense that
'It was dark'

The Bridge

She took out her bike to start pedaling,
out onto the street racing past homes and people
People she loved and those who loved her
even racing past her own self, standing there smiling
She pedaled faster and harder,
as fast as she could
Making sure, not to pause
so she could make it far
As far as she could, before falling apart
As she reached full speed, she stopped,
paused to breathe looking back
All that was there behind was merely a bridge
One made of memories, so compact that they felt real
She then looked ahead
Ahead of her was another one,
more magnificent than the last one
On the other side, was a glimpse
A glimpse of her own self, waiting
with a brighter smile.

Her Love

What is love for you?
Love is when I got a lot to say, but can't say a
word when I see him
Love is acting like I don't miss him, when all I
want is to be with him
Love is when his ambitions and dreams are
mine too
Love is when he's my happy place
Love is letting someone else be his love if he
wishes to
Love is when I don't confess to let him focus
Love is wanting to ensure and protect his little
heart when I'm not
Love is showing him my ugliest parts,
unfiltered
Love is loving him enough, for the both of us.

The Giver

She was a Giver
She gave love to those who needed
More of it to those who needed it but never
asked
She gave Kindness to everyone
Everyone of those she touched on her way
to heal parts of people and the world
The world called her 'Crazy'
Crazy for wanting to believe,
that the world needs 'her kind' to be 'kind'
Crazy she was, as she counted herself out,
from the world she wanted to heal
She who forgot 'self-love',
Was ready to give 'herself' to the world
She with no one to fix her,
was ready to fix her world.

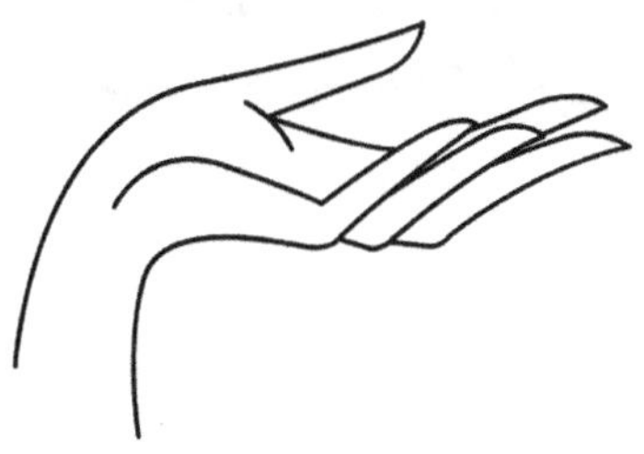

His Love

"What do you love about her ?" someone asked
"Her beautiful eyes,
those eyes which sometimes rain when her lips get
heavy with secrets,
the secrets she kept sealed,
tight shut in her heart
Her heart, found always on her sleeve
Her soul with gates, guarded by walls
Built higher each time, with bricks
Bricks of pain plastered with the shattered pieces of
her
Her smile, bright, in hopes of hiding the burden
better
Her hair, with luscious locks layered and full of life,
just like her
Her arms, full and warm
as warm as the insides of her soft soul
Most importantly, the soft scent of the lingering
words every time she spoke"
He replied.